WORLD RECORD BREAKERS

THE WORLD'S DEADLIEST ANIMALS

BY SEAN STEWART PRICE

Consultant:
Bernd Heinrich, Ph.D, Professor Emeritus
Biology Department, University of Vermont, USA

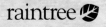

raintree

a Capstone company — publishers for children

Raintree is an imprint of Capstone Global Library Limited, a company incorporated in England and Wales having its registered office at 264 Banbury Road, Oxford, OX2 7DY – Registered company number: 6695582

www.raintree.co.uk
myorders@raintree.co.uk

Edited by Mandy Robbins
Designed by Sarah Bennett
Picture research by Morgan Walters
Production by Laura Manthe
Printed and bound in China.

ISBN 978-1-4747-1158-6
21 20 19 18 17
10 9 8 7 6 5 4 3 2 1

British Library Cataloguing in Publication Data
A full catalogue record for this book is available from the British Library.

Acknowledgements
We would like to thank the following for permission to reproduce photographs: Shutterstock: Alta Oosthuizen, 18, Amee Cross, Cover, Audrey Snider-Bell, top 23, DEmax, design element, Dennis W. Donohue, 10, Dr Morley Read, 11, Eky Studio, design element, FotoYakov, design element, Henrik Larsson, 26, Hugh Lansdown, 15, jeep2499, 21, john michael evan potter, 17, 20, Juan Gaertner, 29, Kristian Bell, 9, Marco Uliana, 27, Mogens Trolle, 25, O lympus, 7, Orhan Cam, bottom 23, reptiles4all, 5, Seraphim Art, design element, Volodymyr Burdiak, 19, Wiktoria Pawlak, design element, YUSRAN ABDUL RAHMAN, 13

Every effort has been made to contact copyright holders of material reproduced in this book. Any omissions will be rectified in subsequent printings if notice is given to the publisher.

CONTENTS

PRIMAL FEAR

Coming face to face with a lion. Hearing a snake's cold hiss and seeing its fangs dripping **venom**. Running into the web of a **poisonous** spider. People are naturally frightened of these things. Early humans lived in fear of dangerous animals attacking them.

Today animal attacks aren't a major concern for most people. In fact, humans are much more dangerous to animals overall. Through hunting and crowding out natural habitats, animals are in danger more than ever before. But animals can still be deadly to humans. Animals are responsible for thousands of deaths and millions of injuries each year. Sometimes these dangerous encounters occur at unexpected times or in surprising ways.

WARNING!

Animals usually don't attack unless they feel threatened. If you think an animal might be dangerous, leave it alone. Never try to pick up, pet or catch a wild animal.

FACT

When it comes to the deadliest animal in the world, you've probably already been attacked by it. Keep reading to find out what it is.

venom liquid poison made by an animal to kill its prey

poisonous able to kill or harm if swallowed, inhaled or sometimes even touched

CHAPTER 1

POISONOUS CREEPY CRAWLIES

Animals use poisons for two reasons: to kill **prey** and to fight off **predators**. Many scientists say there is a big difference between animals that are venomous and those that are poisonous. Venomous animals include certain snakes and spiders. They inject a victim with venom. Poisonous animals include some frogs and fish. People become sick by touching or eating them. Basically, if it bites you and you get sick, the animal is venomous. If you bite it and get sick, it is poisonous. Other scientists argue that all venoms are just poisons. So when you say a snake is poisonous, you're not wrong. But saying it's venomous is more accurate.

ANTIVENOM

Doctors have medicines to treat most venomous bites and stings. They are called antivenom. Antivenom is made by gathering venom from animals. That poison is used to create a medicine that counters the deadly effects of venom.

prey animal hunted by another animal as food
predator animal that hunts other animals for food

Komodo dragons are found only on a few Indonesian islands.

KOMODO DRAGON

The world's largest lizard lives on five islands in the Pacific Ocean. It can grow up to 3 metres (10 feet) long. The jaws holding its curved, jagged teeth can bite off a leg and easily tear flesh. Scientists once thought Komodo bites left deadly bacteria that could kill anyone able to escape an attack. But in 2009 they found out that the truth might be worse. Komodo bites leave a slow-acting venom in the victims that takes days to kill. Despite their fearsomeness, Komodo dragons have only attacked 12 people in the last 35 years.

SNAKES

About 3,000 snake species exist today. Around 600 are venomous. Each year venomous snakes kill about 100,000 people. They also permanently disable 250,000 people.

The king cobra of South Asia has a terrifying hiss. It sounds like a dog growling. One bite has enough venom to kill an elephant or 20 people.

The common lancehead of Central and South America is aggressive. This snake often kills people even with antivenom treatment.

In Australia the eastern brown snake is the snake that kills the most people. But the taipan has a more deadly attack. Before antivenom was developed in the 1950s, taipan bites were 100 per cent deadly. Taipans usually flee instead of attacking someone, though.

Many experts believe the saw-scaled viper of Africa has the most deadly snake venom. These snakes kill more people in Africa than all the other African snakes combined.

FACT

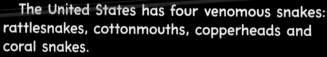

The United States has four venomous snakes: rattlesnakes, cottonmouths, copperheads and coral snakes.

HOW DANGEROUS ARE SNAKEBITES?

In wealthy countries, good medical care means you have a better chance of being struck by lightning than dying of snakebite. But in sub-Saharan Africa, about 1.5 million people are bitten by snakes each year. About 20,000 die because of poor access to medical care.

Saw-scaled vipers are common in many parts of Africa and the Middle East.

DANGEROUS SPIDERS

The Brazilian wandering spider is widely considered the world's deadliest spider. It hides in corners and tight spaces and has very potent venom. Small children are at the most risk of dying. Deaths are now rare thanks to antivenom.

The false widow is the most venomous spider in the UK. This spider heads indoors when weather cools. It likes to hide in dark spaces and isn't aggressive but it will bite when threatened. Bites are rare but painful. They result in blisters, burns, and ugly welts on the skin. No deaths have been attributed to the false widow.

THE DEATHSTALKER

Out of 1,500 scorpion species, 50 are dangerous to humans. The most dangerous is the deathstalker, found in the Middle East and North Africa. Anyone stung by a deathstalker will feel extreme pain, have **convulsions** and become **paralyzed**. They may die of heart or **respiratory** failure if they don't get antivenom soon.

Deathstalkers can have bright yellow colouring.

For every person killed by a venomous snake, 10 are killed by a venomous scorpion.

Leg spans for the Brazilian wandering spider can reach up to 15 centimetres (6 inches).

convulsion uncontrollable jerking of the muscles

paralyzed having lost the ability to control muscles

respiratory related to the process of breathing

CHAPTER 2

POISONOUS SEA CREATURES

Many poisonous animals live on land, but some of the deadliest are swimming in the world's oceans.

BLUE-RINGED OCTOPUS

This golf ball-sized creature may have the deadliest venom on Earth. Just one blue-ringed octopus has enough poison in its saliva to kill 26 people. There is no antivenom. The only way to survive is with hours of heart massage until the poison has worked its way out of a person's body. The good news is that attacks by blue-ringed octopuses are very rare. Only three people have died from them in the past 100 years.

BOX JELLYFISH

Most beach-goers know to stay away from jellyfish. But the box jellyfish is in a league of its own. Its venom is so painful that humans can go into shock and drown. Others die of heart failure before getting back to shore. Those who survive a box jellyfish sting don't forget it. The pain can last for weeks, and the tentacles leave deep scars.

The blue-ringed octopus got its name from the bright blue rings on its skin.

FACT

The puffer fish carries the same type of poison as the blue-ringed octopus. In some countries puffer fish meat is a delicacy. In Japan between 30 and 50 people per year are sent to the hospital for puffer fish poisoning. As many as six of them die as a result.

CHAPTER 3

ALLERGY ATTACK

No one wants to get stung by a poisonous insect. But for some people, stings are more than just painful. They can be deadly.

BEES AND WASPS

Though they're relatively small, bees and wasps can be quite dangerous to people. Some bees – such as Africanized killer bees – can be aggressive and attack suddenly in groups. But that's not the real problem. About two people out of every 1,000 are allergic to bee and wasp stings. Just one sting can make an allergic person very ill or even cause death.

DON'T KILL BEES AND WASPS!

Despite the dangers, bees and wasps are very helpful. Bees **pollinate** the plants that make about one-third of the world's food grow. Wasps control other pests. Don't kill them just because you're afraid.

pollinate transfer pollen from plant to plant; pollen makes new plants grow

FACT

Every year, an average of five people die from bee and wasp stings in the UK.

BULLET ANTS

It's no secret that venomous bites and stings can really hurt. The Schmidt Sting Pain Index rates the pain of insect stings. Its creator, Justin Schmidt, rated the sting of Central and South America's bullet ant as one of the most painful. He said it's "like walking over flaming charcoal with a 3-inch [7.6-centimetre] nail embedded in your heel." Though their stings are very painful, bullet ants are not deadly to most humans. Only people with an allergy to the bullet ant venom are in serious danger from their sting.

A bullet ant is the largest ant in the world.

SCHMIDT STING PAIN INDEX
Level 4: bullet ant, tarantula hawk wasp
Level 3: paper wasp, harvester ant
Level 2: honey bee, yellow jacket wasp, bald-faced hornet
Level 1: fire ant, sweat bee

CHAPTER 4

PURE POWER

Humans are the world's top predator. Their intelligence and physical abilities allow them to outfox or overpower most animals. But when a human faces a lion, bear or shark, don't bet on the human winning the battle. Brute strength will win the fight. There are many powerful animals in the world. Their strength makes them extremely deadly. Even the biggest wild animals don't hunt humans. But they don't always like us hanging around.

ELEPHANTS

African and Asian elephants are the largest land mammals on Earth. They also travel in herds. Chances are, if you make one angry, you'll probably get trampled. In India alone, Asian elephants kill up to 300 people per year.

Young elephants stay with their mothers for 16 years – almost as long as humans!

DECLINING WILD ANIMAL POPULATION

Though humans fear dangerous wild animals, there are fewer to fear than there once were. Many wild animal populations are declining. Human construction has destroyed habitats. Over-hunting has killed a large number of majestic creatures. For example, over the last 100 years African elephant populations have dropped from about 5 million to nearly 470,000. Similar drops have been seen in other large animals, such as lions, tigers, cougars and alligators. Some, like the Asian snow leopard, are **endangered**.

endangered at risk of dying out

CAPE BUFFALO

Cape buffalo are grazing animals that look big and slow. But an adult male can charge at 56 kilometres (35 miles) per hour. A charging buffalo can overturn a car or kill a lion with its sharp horns. Cape buffalo are responsible for at least 200 human deaths a year.

RHINOCEROSES

Like cape buffalo, rhinos are big, unpredictable and easy to anger. Rhinos have poor vision, so they tend to charge first and ask questions later. A rhino has a deadly horn that can be more than 0.46 metre (1.5 feet) long.

The horns of male cape buffalo are larger than those of females.

WEIGHT COMPARISONS

Average human male	Average pickup truck	African elephant	cape buffalo	rhinoceros
82 kilograms (180 pounds)	2,495 kilograms (5,500 pounds)	2,267 to 6,350 kilograms (5,000 to 14,000 pounds)	408 to 861 kilograms (900 to 1,900 pounds)	1,406 to 3,583 kilograms (3,100 to 7,900 pounds)

FACT

White rhinos are on the verge of **extinction**, mostly from illegal hunting.

extinction no longer living; an extinct animal is one that has died out

LIONS

Hunting and habitat destruction have reduced the number of lions. But they are still common in parts of Africa, where they are an important part of the food chain. In those places, lions can still be a menace when their food supply is low. Lions account for as many as 250 human deaths each year.

Lions are typically at the top of the food chain. Any animal – including humans – can be prey.

TIGERS

In December 2014 several people died in tiger attacks in villages in northern India. Tigers don't often attack people, so that meant one thing. The tigers' normal prey of buffalo, deer and wild pigs was in short supply. Tigers kill fewer than 85 people each year. They are an endangered animal, which means they are protected. Though it's illegal, many people kill tigers for their valuable fur or to keep them from killing people.

Wild tigers are found in parts of Asia.

BEARS

Bears are so big and strong that even guns may not stop their attacks. But bears seldom attack people unless they feel threatened or if someone is invading their territory. They may also attack hunters carrying fresh meat. In North America, there is usually less than one death per year from bear attacks.

CHAPTER 5

PREDATORS IN THE WATER

Bodies of water may look beautiful or even calm, but great dangers may be lurking beneath the surface. When it comes to wild animals, you're more likely to get into trouble near water.

HIPPOPOTAMUSES

Cartoons often make hippos seem like jolly animals. Don't be fooled. Hippos kill more humans than any other large animal in Africa. They are very protective and can run up to 32 kilometres (20 miles) per hour. Their canine teeth reach up to 51 centimetres (20 inches). That kind of power can easily kill.

CROCODILES AND ALLIGATORS

Big teeth. Strong jaws. Great at hide-and-seek. What's not to fear about alligators and crocodiles? One minute you're walking along a riverbank, and the next, you're getting dragged underwater. Luckily, attacks by crocs and gators are rare – even for people who live near them. More importantly, most attacks are not fatal. In the last 60 years Florida alligators have caused just 18 deaths in the United States.

Can you spot the differences betwee
this crocodile and the alligators belo

ALLIGATORS VS. CROCODILES

ALLIGATOR	CROCODILE
Found in: United States, Central and South America, China	**Found in:** Africa, Asia and North and South America
Habitat: freshwater swamps, lakes, slow-moving streams	**Habitat:** freshwater and saltwate areas
Bodies: jaws shaped like a U; only upper teeth visible when mouth closed	**Bodies:** jaws shaped like a V; upper and lower teeth visible when mouth closed

THE NOT-SO-DEADLY PIRANHA

Horror films have shown piranhas as flesh-eating monsters. These fish can kill people, and they can be dangerous. But generally, they leave people alone unless they smell blood from an open wound. Piranhas almost never swarm the way it's shown in films. People might get bitten or lose a finger in a serious attack. Otherwise, piranhas usually only attack the bodies of people who have already drowned.

GREAT WHITE SHARK

The film *Jaws* gave great white sharks a reputation as killing machines. Great white sharks are very deadly animals – if you're a seal or a penguin. They do sometimes kill humans. But humans usually aren't on the menu for sharks. In most years, fewer than a dozen people are killed by all sharks – not just great whites.

FACT

Piranhas often make a barking sound when caught by people fishing.

Great white sharks can swim 40 kilometres (25 miles) per hour in short bursts.

THE WAR ON SHARKS

Sharks do kill people, but it's probably because they mistake them for other animals. On the other hand, humans kill thousands of sharks. People kill sharks mostly for food and for sport. Human activities also destroy shark habitats and kill the fish sharks eat. For these reasons, many types of sharks are now threatened with extinction.

CHAPTER 6

DEADLY VECTORS

So which animal is the deadliest to humans? Believe it or not, it's the mighty mosquito! That may not have been the answer you were expecting. That's because many people don't understand how mosquitoes kill. Mosquitoes are vectors. A vector is an animal that carries a disease from person to person or place to place. Most are blood-sucking insects. Mosquitoes are the world's deadliest vector. They spread malaria, West Nile virus and the Zika virus. Malaria kills 600,000 people each year. Most of them are children under five.

Female mosquitoes are the only mosquitoes that bite.

FACT

Big animals can also be vectors. Dogs are one of the biggest vectors for spreading rabies.

TSETSE FLIES

The mosquito is not the only insect that spreads deadly diseases. The tsetse fly is another vector. It transmits a terrible disease called sleeping sickness. It kills about 10,000 people a year, mostly in Africa.

Most assassin bugs are black, brown or grey, but some can be brightly coloured.

ASSASSIN BUG

The well-named assassin bug spreads a disease called Chagas. Many of its victims are in Mexico. Chagas is responsible for about 10,000 deaths each year.

CHAPTER 7

THE PREDATORS INSIDE

A **parasite** is an organism that lives on or in a host. It gets its food from or at the expense of its host. Most parasites are harmless or even helpful. For instance, there are bacteria in your stomach that you can't live without. If those bacteria weren't there, you couldn't **digest** your food. But other parasites are predators that attack us from inside. In fact, many deadly illnesses are caused by parasites.

TINY KILLERS WHO WORK FOR US

Something interesting happens when people cut the number of parasites they're exposed to. They become more likely to get other types of diseases that attack the immune system. This includes common problems such as asthma and allergies. Doctors have found that they can actually treat certain diseases by deliberately giving people intestinal worms. They may be helpful for treating serious diseases such as multiple sclerosis. But these treatments are done in a controlled way. No one should ever deliberately give themselves worms.

parasite animal or plant that lives on or inside another animal or plant and causes harm

digest break down food so it can be used by the body

28

WORMS

When you think about worms, earthworms probably come to mind. But some worms are parasites. They feed directly on other animals over a long period of time. The tapeworm, for instance, gets into people's food and then

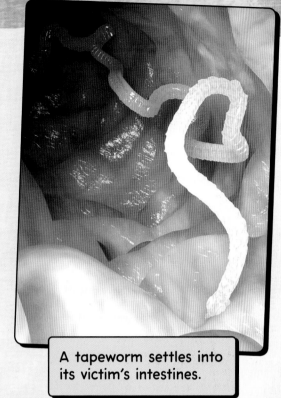

A tapeworm settles into its victim's intestines.

lives in their stomachs. The tapeworm consumes food so the person becomes much weaker. Tapeworms kill about 2,000 people each year. That's far more than the number of people killed each year by crocodiles.

We share our world with millions of other creatures. Big or small, these creatures can pose a risk to us. Be smart and respectful of animals, and you'll probably be fine. You are, after all, the number one predator on the planet.

GLOSSARY

antivenom medicine that cures people of poisonous animal bites or stings

convulsion uncontrollable jerking of the muscles

digest break down food so it can be used by the body

endangered at risk of dying out

extinction no longer living; an extinct animal is one that has died out

paralyzed having lost the ability to control muscles

parasite animal or plant that lives on or inside another animal or plant and causes harm

poisonous able to kill or harm if swallowed, inhaled or sometimes even touched

pollinate transfer pollen from plant to plant; pollen makes new plants grow

predator animal that hunts other animals for food

prey animal hunted by another animal as food

respiratory related to the process of breathing

vector animal that carries a disease from person to person or place to place

venom liquid poison made by an animal to kill its prey

FIND OUT MORE

BOOKS

Animal Record Breakers, Steve Parker (Carlton Books, 2013)

Deadliest Annual 2016, Steve Backshall (Orion Children's Books, 2015)

The World's Weirdest Animals (Library of Weird), Lindsy O'Brien (Raintree, 2016)

WEBSITES

Kids Travel Cam: Dangerous Animals
www.kidstravelcam.co.uk/kids-travel-guide/worlds-most-dangerous-animals/

National Geographic: Deadly 60
animals.nationalgeographic.com/animals/wild/shows-deadly-60/pictures/

UK Safari
www.uksafari.com/index.htm

COMPREHENSION QUESTIONS

1. Why might you be more at risk of coming into contact with a dangerous animal in the water as opposed to on land?

2. Why might a smaller, weaker animal be more dangerous than a larger, stronger animal?

INDEX